UNCONDITIONAL THOUGHTS

WILL RASMUSSEN

CONTENTS

Acknowledgments   7

A Man Like Me   9
Accomplish   10
Always There   11
Around This Place   12
Back at The Beginning   14
Back Stab   17
Broken Bat   18
Broke In Two   20
Care for You   22
CJR   23
Clear Mind   25
Closed Circle   27
Come Back   28
Come Home   30
Intro to Consumption of Life   32
Consumption of Life   33
Cut Ties   35
Do You Know   37
Don't Make Sense   38
Dreams   39
Empty   40
Excuses   42
Eye to Eye   43
Intro to Fakebook   44
Fakebook   45
Fall in Love   47
Fight   48
For You   49
For Your Love   50
Friend   51
Grow   53
Humble   54

Hurts Inside	55
Intro to I Can Only See You in My Dreams	56
I Can Only See You in My Dreams	57
I Don't Have the Answers	59
I Loved Her	60
I See You	61
I Want to Be	62
If I Were to Cry	63
In My Past	65
In the End	67
Keep Going	69
KJR	70
Intro to Letter to Future Me	73
Letter to Future Me	74
Letter to Past Me	76
Lies	78
Lonely Heart	80
Lost	81
Make Me Cry	82
Meet	83
Mind Block	84
Intro to Mom	86
Mom	87
Need to Change	89
Noise	91
Not Equal	93
Not Just Your Beauty	95
Not the Girl for Me	97
Not What It Seems	99
Only Be Me	101
Only See You	103
Over	105
Past to Future	107
Perfect Place	109
Pick Me Apart	110
PJR	112
Please Stay	114
Rewind Time	115
Simple Things	116
Soul	118
Stand Still	120

Stay in Love	122
Superman	123
Tears in Your Eyes	125
That Night	127
The One	129
Things Aren't the Same	131
Torn	133
Travel the World	134
Turn Your Back	136
Types of Friends	138
Unconditional Thoughts	140
What Would Life Be Like	141
What Went Wrong	143
What You've Made Me	145
Wishful Thinking	146
Words	147
Would You Mind	148
Would You Mind Part 2	150
You're in Charge	152
You're the Girl	153
About the Author	155

Unconditional Thoughts copyrighted 2020 by Will Rasmussen.

All rights reserved. No part of this publication may be reproduced or transmitted in any form or by any means, without the permission in writing from the publisher.

❧ Created with Vellum

ACKNOWLEDGMENTS

Wow I can finally say that one of my biggest dreams have come true. You are holding in your hands over 26 years of all original poems that have come straight from my heart. Unconditional Thoughts is a realism, emotional roller coaster into my world written in poem form. There is no way I could have written this book without some very influential people that I consider close to me.

    First and foremost, I'd like to thank my creator in heaven, God. If not for Him I wouldn't have been blessed with this gift of writing poetry. I wouldn't be able to breath the air that I breath.

    The second person on my list to thank is my mother. Without a doubt she is the strongest women I know. My mom busted her butt day and night to make sure my brother and I were always taken care of. I'm not sure what I would do without my mom. I hope she knows I love her with all my heart.

    I would like to thank my grandmother who I miss every day of my life. I could talk to my grandmother about anything and everything and she seemed to always have the right answers no matter what issue I would bring to her. I love you grandma and I will see you again someday.

    To my beautiful amazing wife, Lindsey who puts up with me every day all day. I love you more than words can say. I hit the lotto when I met and married you. My wife is the artist of the back cover of the book. She drew that picture because I'm always dancing and being silly. The picture is very dear to my heart.

The amazing cover photo of the book was drawn by someone I consider my brother, Aaron Robinson. It was Aaron who gave me the chance to write articles for his magazine Consciousness. He saw something in me that I didn't see, for that I thank you my friend.

These next three guys on my list to thank have all been mentors to me at some time in my life. Emanuel Jackson and Gabe Wright, I met you two while attending Olivet Nazarene University. I can say you guys pulled me out of a dark place when I met you both. I consider you guys my friends for life, and I thank you for being there for me when I needed it most. A man I consider my big brother, Christian Davis, our trip to Atlanta is one I will never forget. You have always given me sound advice, and for that I say thank you.

Thanks in advance to everyone that is about to take time out of their day to read this.

Peace and Love to all
    Will Rasmussen

A MAN LIKE ME

I sometimes wonder
If you could love a man like me
Someone who's tranquilizing
Someone who's reassuring
Someone who will guard and protect you right
Someone who can love you at first sight
Someone who would go the extra mile just to see you smile
Someone that will hold you tight in the harsh night
Someone that would yearn to make you laugh
Someone that might even make you cry
That someone is a man like me
Could you love a man like me
One of these days
I hope that you can see
That man is right here
Waiting to love you unconditionally
Even if you can't fantasize
Loving a man like me

ACCOMPLISH

What is it in life that you crave
What are your deepest desires
Would you sell your soul
To obtain these possessions
Or can you achieve
These conditions through
Genuine devotion
The truth is
You can have what you want
You just need to put your heart and soul into it
Defy all the odds
Don't struggle with uncertainty
Don't allow yourself to fail
Push through negativity and conflict
Devote yourself to your aspirations
And relish in your success
Because you truly can
Achieve all you aspire for

ALWAYS THERE

With the concluding farewells
It is only a temporary goodbye
I'm in paradise now
I'll contemplate our next embrace
For what will seem like eternity
I long for your warm smile
I anticipate our next conversation
Reminiscing on our mortality
Don't be somber
Cause I'm always nearby
My presence is constant
Whether you feel it or not
Even though my mortal being has perished
My spirit lives in your heart
Until we meet again
I'll prevail as your guardian angel
Until we rejoice in eternal life

AROUND THIS PLACE

I was raised where my neighborhood felt more like family
That familiar face became my haven
Reminiscing on the innocent opportunities
It's where I was constructed
It is my foundation
And if I could turn back
The hands of time
I don't think I would leave
I had a dream
About moving to LA
But I've been there three times
In my lifetime
Now I love visiting LA
But everything out there
Moves too fast for me
You see my hometown
Is not fast paced at all
And I'm more of a laid back
Type of fella
The main reason I wouldn't
Have left my hometown

Is I wouldn't have met
My amazing wife
If that wouldn't have happened
Then I wouldn't have the amazing three kids that I have
My life would have been
Totally different
And, I would not
Trade my current life for anything

BACK AT THE BEGINNING

Let's take a little journey
Back to the beginning
When you and I first met
To me it's an interesting story
You see we both worked
At the same hospital
Provena St Mary's to be exact
You knew about me
And I sometimes seen you in passing
My cousin gave you my screen name
On messenger and out of the blue
You messaged me
We messaged each other for about a year
Suddenly you just disappeared
One night in November
I seen you were online
I sent you a message
Just to say hi
You were working on a paper
For a college course
You said you needed help

You invited me over
I didn't have anything going on
So, I drove to Ashkum
I arrived at your house
And we worked on the paper
We talked through the night
And before I knew it
The time said two in the morning
I decided to leave you
And you asked if you could come with
I said sure why not
Let's keep this party going
Back at my house
We attempted to watch Varsity Blues
My eyes were getting heavy
So, I told you I was going to snooze
You ended up staying the night
I slept in my bed
You slept on my sofa
When morning arrived, we made plans
To hang out later that night
Our first date we went
To Aurelio's Pizza
Your friend Kristin worked there
And she was our server
Our next date was to Chicago
It was the middle of December
I thought I was a tough guy
And I only wore a hoodie
We were inseparable right from the start
Christmas rolled around
And you decorated my house
Christmas Eve came, and we were apart
But first thing Christmas morning
You were at my door step
New Year's Eve you moved in with me

I got off work early that night
And was going to surprise you
But when I came through the back door
You almost stabbed me in the chest
I proposed to you on your birthday
Shortly after that
Surprise Kindall was cooking in your belly
We got married in 2011
Took a honeymoon cruise
To the Caribbean
Then came Preston
Our second child
And by this time
We were ready for a bigger house
Caitlyn came after Preston
And she is our last child
I ended up going to the Dr.
And getting the kid making tool fixed
Fast forward to present day
And you and I are still a pair
Our relationship isn't all rainbows and roses
But for the most part
We make a good pair
I'm grateful you're my wife
From the beginning to now
I loved you then
I love you even more now

BACK STAB

We were supposed to be friends
At least that's what I thought
Until you showed your true colors
And stabbed me in the heart
You felt no remorse
Talking about me
Behind my back
And when I confronted you about it
You just shrugged your shoulders
And laughed
But I thought we were close
I told you things
That no one else knew
Well I learned my lesson
And I must confess
That I let my guard down
But I can guarantee you this
It damn sure won't
Happen again

BROKEN BAT

Batman has been fighting all night
He's exhausted and dehydrated
He thinks he has
A cracked rib or two
Cause every time
He takes a deep breath
It hurts something fierce
He's been fighting non-stop
For about a week now
He's locked all his rouge gallery back up
That had been broke out of Arkham
He is finally heading home
When he reaches the Batcave
Something isn't right
Alfred his butler and friend
Doesn't greet him
Like he usually does every night
When he parks the Batmobile
And he gets out of the car
Standing in his sight
Is a villain named Bane

And Batman knows right away
This could be the fight of his life
He pulls his cowl down onto his face
And he charges towards Bane
Batman is met with a fist to his face
His head beings to ring
He is so tired
That he knowns this isn't going
To be much of a fight
But he must try to stop this monster with all his might
He hits Bane with a left, then with a right
But Bane seems unfazed, Bane is ready for this fight
Bane lefts the caped crusader up over his head
And slams him down on his knee
Batman's back hits so hard
You can hear it snap right in half
Bane leaves Batman a broken man
Batman will live to fight again
It just won't be tonight

BROKE IN TWO

Your radiant smile can light up a room
You have a personality
That people would pay a million bucks for
But even with these great qualities
Your heart is still broken in two
It has been ripped out of your chest
And stepped on
Right in front of you
Whoever did this to you
Deserves to be slapped
It isn't too late
For your heart to be healed
That door hasn't closed yet
Just refuse to walk through it
No matter how much it pains you
Try not to let negativity
Control your mind anymore
Surround yourself with positive people
That will raise you up
When you are down
They can be that shoulder

You can cry on
You're too great of a person
To be down in the dumps
Just keep reminding yourself
To never give up

CARE FOR YOU

How can I manifest to you
How much I cherish your presence
What can I do
To convey to you
I'll be devoted to you
I can invest in heartfelt endeavors
I can take you
On lavish travels
In the Caribbean
But reassuring you, encouraging you, and supporting you
Might be a more desiring aspiration
I could confess I love you
Not displayed in a verse
I could welcome your hand into mine
We can weather any storm
Elevating you every chance I get
Sounds oh so admirable
But granting you all my sentiments
Is how I'll display
My passion for you

CJR

You are the last
Of my three children
When your mom told me, she was pregnant
With you it was a total surprise
I almost had a heart attack
And I didn't believe your mom at that time
I wasn't sure how we were going to
Raise another kid
Let alone the two we already had
You're real close in age to your brother
And that really scared me
We found out you were a girl
And I thought holy smokes
I'm going to have to raise two girls
You were born in January just like me
Your birthday is two days after me
We named you Caitlyn June
You were as cute as a button
And once again with the arrival of you
Our now family of five
Out grew our homestead

Your mom and I decided to build
Our dream house in a cul-de-sac
Your personality is for sure one of a kind
Your sassy and precious
All at the same time
Your turning into a big girl
Because I was for sure you would
Have a meltdown at daycare
Being's your brother was no longer there
But instead it was the complete opposite
You weren't upset at all
That big bro wasn't there
To play with you
Your coming into your own
And you will be ready
To take on the world for sure
Your mom and I love you very much
And with every day that passes
We are so proud you are our daughter

CLEAR MIND

I got one shot
At this roller coaster
Called life
I've put myself
Through some harsh
Mental beatings
I've now cleared
My cloudy mind
I focus my mind
On positive stuff
No more negativity
No more complaining
And no more excuses
I now realize
This whole time
That the person who was holding me back
Was none other than me
I'm now on the right track
I got some big things
In the works

I'll never stand in my own way
Ever again

CLOSED CIRCLE

I try to keep
My circle of friends limited
Preventing many from getting
Close to me
The logic for this
Is trust
You see I must know
Your down with me
Through thick and thin
I need to know you'll ride with me
Through the good times and bad
I don't loath on fruitless endeavors
I just won't stand for it
My circle of friends knows this
We all try to stay cognizant
My circle of friends
Would be there for me
As I would be there for them
I choose my friends sparingly
Because I know
Just how detrimental bad ones are

COME BACK

Let go of all the things that bind you
Take a walk with me
I'll help guide you
Down a path that will set you free
A path that you need to see
That path you're on right now
Is full of destruction and pain
It leaves you crying yourself
Right to sleep
If that's the path you wish to stay on
I can guaranty you this
Because we are friends
I will not let you
Go down this path
You deserve to be happy
Not all sad and depressed
I'm not saying I have all the answers
All I know is
I want my friend back
The one who used to smile

The one who used to love
The one who was great to be around
The one who just had fun
Come back, my friend
It's not too late

COME HOME

What happens to a man
That has strayed from God's path
When arrogance takes over
Confidence consumes his character
With his righteous morality in question
He sends Jesus
To the mountain to pray and anticipate
That this man could return someday
But Jesus takes exception
He stays right in the man's footpath
As the man continued to do things
His own way
Jesus kept vigilant
As everything the man did became fruitless
With having lost his friends, money, and loved ones
The man finally calls out
To the one person who could help
He yells, Jesus what have I done to deserve this turmoil in my life
Jesus responded
My son you left your course
I prepared for you

You abandoned me
Yet during times of suffering and grief
I never left you
I will never relinquish my love for you
I'll just sit and wait for you to return to my grace

INTRO TO CONSUMPTION OF LIFE

I asked my friend one day what they thought I should write about. Their response was how about life being so busy that there seems to never be enough time in the day for yourself. I thought wow that would be an interesting poem to write. When I sat down to write Consumption of Life my pencil just flowed across the page. The poem seemed easy for me to write because everyone can relate, including myself. I feel it is important for everyone to take some time to just be by themselves. We all get caught up in life, and if you don't take time for yourself, life can drive you mad. I let my friend, who gave me the idea, read the poem and they gave me their approval. I hope you to enjoy Consumption of Life.

CONSUMPTION OF LIFE

In life
You can find yourself
Being consumed
With work, laundry, dishes
Your kid's volleyball games
Baseball games, football
Even swim meets
There is homework and bills
Let's not forget pleasing your spouse
If you have one
If you're a single parent
Your load can be greater
All this stuff consumes your life
To the point where you
Lose your identity
You become lost in your mundane endeavors
Do you even know who you are becoming
Do you truly ever stop evolving
Have you asked yourself recently
What legacy do you want to leave
Have you allowed yourself time

To reflect on your life's priorities
Your perspective in life may change
Yeah, I get that
What I'm trying to say
Is are you staying true to yourself
Or are you letting life consume who you are
Find that balance
Between doing your daily duties
And spending time by yourself
Please don't discredit the importance of self-meditation
To relieve
These consumptions of life

CUT TIES

It's easier said than done
To let go of things
That are holding us back
We are drawn to these things like they are magnets
Whether it be friends, family members, or addictions
We try so hard
To just walk away
But we find ourselves
Being sucked back into the pain
There's no easy solution
But to want to change
Tell yourself you deserve better
Then turn and walk the other way
Cause once you let go
Of what's holding you back
Your full potential can shine through
You'll have the strength to bounce back
I know it's going to be hard
I know it may suck
But try cutting ties

With whatever is causing you pain
Cut ties with whatever is holding you back
And get your life
Back on the right track

DO YOU KNOW

Do you know I care for you
Do you know I'll always be there for you
Do you know I'll listen attentively to you
Do you know I'll walk alongside you
Do you know I'll wipe every tear from your eyes
Do you know I'll support your decisions
Because I cherish you
I don't think you'll ever know
Just how much
I love you

DON'T MAKE SENSE

You don't know me
So, you say
You may be right
But you just talked to me yesterday
You despise me
So, you say
Well that's funny
You just kissed me the other day
You don't want to associate with me
So, you say
Now that's laughable
Because just Tuesday
You told me you loved me
We can't be together
So, you say
Well I say
You had me caught on every word
And I'm telling you today
You're just a fraud
So, you can turn
And walk right out that door

DREAMS

Dreams can be happy
Dreams can allow you to mourn
Dreams can make you joyous
Dreams can be complicated
Dreams can be brief
But there is one prevailing element
We must not discredit a dreams relevance
Dreams are what you make them
For everyone has significance
And your dreams can develop

EMPTY

Why is my soul
So empty inside
Who is willing to take note why
I'm not happy within my heart
And I don't even know
How to morph my mind
That is submerged in my vacant thoughts
I believe in God
I have Faith
Shouldn't that be enough
To take these burdens away
I try to do
Everything just right
Even if I'm wrong
I try to make it right
It's all becoming so overwhelming
I'm slipping into the darkness
I feel emptiness
Closing in
All around me

I'm losing control of
This emptiness inside of me
I must find the loophole
Because I can't stand
All this that has confined me

EXCUSES

Excuses we make them
About everything
That's what we do
We are human beings
Excuses help us live a fair tale
Excuses help us run from our issues that are real
Excuses are an easy way out
Excuses are ways to let people we love down
Excuses can hold us back from reaching our full potential
Excuses can put strain on your heart
And make you die quicker
Take all your excuses
Roll them in a ball
And throw them to the side
You don't need them anymore
Go ahead and fight this excuses fight
Just try it with all your might
Don't let excuses
Ruin your life

EYE TO EYE

We seem to be deviating from
Each other's ambitions
We are becoming egotistical
Our monopoly is collapsing
Because we are navigating through
A different prospective
When we find our common ground
The inevitable will materializes
But if the misfortune prevails
Devastation will deplete me

INTRO TO FAKEBOOK

I was inspired to write this poem because so many of us live fake lives on social media. It seems easier for us to hide behind social media and paint pictures like everything is fine, when we are hurting inside and need help. We tend hard to please the masses these days. With that said I hope you enjoy reading Fakebook.

FAKEBOOK

Under your profile picture
It says you're in love
Come on now who are you fooling
You and I know what's up
I start to look through your posts
And just the other day
You posted a picture of you and him
Hugged up together
That's funny because just
Five minutes ago, you told me
Your relationship sucked
You told me he verbally abuses you
But he's never hit you
My question to you is
Why are you painting this picture
On Fakebook like your relationship
Is a nice fluffy cloud in the sky
When your miserable inside
It's not my place
To tell you what to do

I can give you my advice
And that would be to leave that zero
Don't sell yourself short
Just because he tells you
He loves you once a month

FALL IN LOVE

What makes a person
Fall in love
If you can answer this question
You would make millions
Is it a certain thing
Or only found in the eye of the beholder
What makes a person
Fall in love
I wish I could answer
This question with words
But there are no words
That can describe the feeling
I encountered when you showed me
There is such a thing
As real love

FIGHT

The world is in danger
It's going to fall into
The hands of a stranger
What is there for humans to do
The world can turn to me
I'll be their superhero
That will defeat evil
The powers that be
Won't be able to hold me back
I'll save the world
And I won't forget about the kids
I'm sure it's going to be a rough fight
But I'll come out swinging
As if I'm Iron Mike
And when the smoke clears
And all the dust settles
I'll be the one left standing
The one who defeated evil

FOR YOU

If you're feeling down
You can count on me
I'll be around
If you feel sad
I'll comfort you
Whenever you're needing to vent
I'll be there
To lend my ear
Whatever problem you may have
I'm here to help
I want you to know
I truly care for you
And I'll always
Be there for you

FOR YOUR LOVE

I wish I could have your
Love right now
I dream of holding you close
Tight in my arms
I would do anything
Just for your love
I'd climb the highest mountain
I'd prevail through any valley
I'd confront my biggest fear
All this and more
I'd do for your love

FRIEND

If you're feeling sad and blue
Let's go take a walk
Here you can lean on my shoulder
Tell me about all your problems
Let me help you solve them
I want you to know
I'm here for you
As a friend
To help you through
You don't have to worry
About going through it alone
Because you're my friend
And I would never leave you
I'm here to lend you
A helping hand
That's what friends are for
To be there when you fall
Pick you up
Dust you off
A true friend is always there

Giving you advice or lending an ear
As a true friend
I will be by your side
Until the end of time

GROW

Do you want to become stagnant
Have pity on your own short comings
Remain stuck in mindless worries
Of tomorrow
Or do you want to thrive
Surrender your doubt
Have faith
In what you have envisioned
You're the only one holding you back
You standing right there
Looking at yourself in that mirror
You see you have all the cards in your hand
You own all the power
Take ownership of your life
Don't stay stuck in that funk
Not when you have so much potential
To be whatever you want

HUMBLE

You let others put you down
You let others stand in your way
This is the story of your life
You live it everyday
They make fun of you
They spit in your face
And all you do
Is say its ok
You always stay humble
You always keep your eyes to the sky
Because you know someday
That the ones who put you down
Will look up to you one day
Because you would have achieved
So much
And they are still
Living their same lives
Bitter and unchanged

HURTS INSIDE

The sadness I feel is debilitating
Why won't you reciprocate what
I feel for you
My suffering is palpable
I will treasure what we had
This love I have heightens my pulse
It's a love that lingers in my soul
You can't doubt my devotion to you
It's evident what we had
Has now dissolved into extinction
Although I hoped you contemplate
Another endeavor
It hurts to know we have reached this point
I dread a day without you
I have become callous because of you
That's what hurts remarkably the most is
The love I have for you will never be affirmed

INTRO TO I CAN ONLY SEE YOU IN MY DREAMS

I mentioned in my acknowledgments how much I love my grandmother. I wrote this poem to honor her for everything she has ever done for me. It took everything in my body to hold back tears while I was writing this poem. This poem is one of my personal favorites in the book and it means so much to me. When my grandmother passed away, I felt like a little part of my entire family passed away also. Grandma was the glue that held the family together. I hope this poem does my grandmother justice, and I hope you enjoy reading I Can Only See You in My Dreams.

I CAN ONLY SEE YOU IN MY DREAMS

I can hear your joyous laugh
I feel your smooth touch
We talk all through the night
But I can tell something isn't right
When I close my eyes
I can see you clear
But when I open my eyes
You are never there
I was just talking to you
And it felt so real
Is this all just another fairy tale
I close my eyes once more
And you're holding out your hand
You ask me how my day went
And I tell you it's been bad
You see something strange is going on
Something I can't wrap my brain around
When I close my eyes
You appear
When I open my eyes
You suddenly disappear

What is going on
Can you give me some answers
Please grandma dear
You glance down at me
And give me a harm smile
You tell me everything is fine
That I should hurry home
Because it is time for supper
I suddenly wake up
Once again, you're not there
It is then I realize
I can only see you in my dreams
For in my heart
And in my dreams
Are the only two places
That you now live

I DON'T HAVE THE ANSWERS

I don't have the answers
To your heavy inquires
I'm not the resolution to your quandary
Because I'm worn from my own trials
There was a time I thought
Your life remedy was precedence
I thought I could give refuge during your hardships
Then I released that
My own welfare needed attention
I have my own rhetorical questions
That need conclusions
I'm not invincible to affliction
I don't have the answers
That you seek
In fact, I have many questions
That I need to find clarity in

I LOVED HER

Her eyes shined
Bright in the luminous night
Her hair
Cascading through the heavens
I loved her
But I couldn't divulge my affection
You left me speechless
And hung up on your elegance
We were effortless
Only to be ripped apart
By another guy
Who hypnotized her heart
Maybe we weren't meant to be
Maybe she never loved me
But all I know
Deep down inside of me
That I truly did love her
Even if she didn't love me

I SEE YOU

I see you
When I blink
I see you
In my deep sleep
There's not one moment in time
When I don't see your face
But it's only in my dreams
That I can see you clearly
For that is the only place
I can hold you near
My heart I want to give you
My love yearns for you
These are the reasons why
I see you
Yes, it's true
All my love
I want to give just to you
I see you
Not just in my dreams
But also, in reality

I WANT TO BE

I want to be the one
You run to at night
I want to be the one
Who holds you so tight
I want to be the one
To make things right
I want to be the one
To take you places that you like
I want to be the one
To hold your hand
I want to be the one
That sometimes you can't stand
I want to be the one
You love tonight
I want to be the one
You love until the end of time

IF I WERE TO CRY

Would you hear me
If I were to cry
Would you wonder
Why I cry
Would you ask me
If everything is alright
If I were to cry
Would you be there for me
In the middle of the night
If I were to cry
Would you reach out to me
To hold me tight
If I were to cry
Would you still be my friend
Tell me to let it all out
And don't be shy
If I were to cry
Would you look at me
As if I were a baby
Or would you say to me

I'm here for you
You're going to be fine
What would happen to us
If I were to cry

IN MY PAST

I come home
After a long day's work
Hoping to see
The women that I love
But all I find
Is a note on the table
Saying goodbye
Maybe I'll see you in the future
I grab the note
With both my hands
I clutch it tight
To my chest
As the note spelled out
That your seeing another man
All of this
I just don't understand
I thought we had a love
That would always last
I see I was wrong
For now, you're just a love

That's going to be
In my past

IN THE END

I used to try so hard
Not to think of you
But when you would leave my mind
I would fall back a step or two
I would journey back into time
When it was you and I
A place I can't get back to
Because you told me goodbye
I thought we were meant to be
But for some foolish reason
You didn't see it this way
You would tell me you love me
But it was all a lie
You were in love with someone else
And I was just too blind
To see the writing on the wall
To see it all come crashing down
At the end of this yellow brick road
There was no pot of gold
And in the end, you hurt my heart

But that was the past
I'll now leave
My past in the dust

KEEP GOING

You can mourn for me
If you like
Stop everything that is going
On in your life
But if this is your choice
Let me tell you this
That is not what I would have wished
Get on with your life
Keep doing all the things
That you like
For if you know it or not
I'm always with you
Always in your mind and your heart
Every time you think of me
I'll be there secretly
Even in times you're not thinking of me
I'll still be looking over your shoulder quietly
I love you and this you know
Until you join me again
You dust yourself off
And keep going

KJR

I remember the day
Like it was yesterday
The day your mother
Told me you were on the way
Your mom and I were afraid
You were going to be our first child
And we really didn't know
How we would raise our
Little bundle of joy
Then it came time
To tell our parents
The news we just received
We didn't know how they would react
But it was time to see
We told grandma and grandpa Altmyer
With great grandma Koch there to
I thought grandpa Altmyer
Was going to ring my neck
It turns out he took the news well
Grandma Altmyer was happy for us

But she was a little disappointed
Great grandma Koch sat in silence
But we knew she was supportive
We told grandma Rasmussen
And she was shocked and happy
All at the same time
All and all everyone were excited
For you to arrive
Then the big day came
And reality set in
Your mom and I
Were really going to be parents
When you arrived
I shed a tear
Because in my arms
I held a beautiful baby girl
That we would name Kindall Jean
As your mom and I
Adjusted to having you in our lives
You were growing up
Right before our eyes
You would scoot around the house on your butt
Because you didn't know how to walk
But when you did finally walk
Oh man you took off
You were in mom's and I's wedding
As our flower girl
And within a blink of an eye
It was time for you to start school
Your first day of school
Was a tough one
You didn't want to go
But you adjusted well
Fast forward to present day
You've turned into a beautiful young lady

You're funny, quiet, and sometimes a little sassy
And you remind me so much of me
Your mom and I love you very much
And with every day that passes
We are so proud to call you our daughter

INTRO TO LETTER TO FUTURE ME

I really had to think long and hard while writing this poem. Writing Letter to Past Me was a piece of cake. This poem challenged me because I have no idea what the future holds for me. I only know how I'd like my future to be, but things don't always work out the way we want. Writing this poem made me realize there are things I do now that I know I could do better or be better at. Writing this was hard I'm not going to lie, but when I was finished, I was pleased with it. I hope you enjoy Letter to Future Me

LETTER TO FUTURE ME

You wrote this letter
In the past
And if you're reading this
There are things in this letter
That would have helped you grow
As a husband, a friend, and dad
First thing you need to do is
Spend as much time
With your kids as you can
They truly do love you
As you do them
Let them know
They can be whatever they want
In this big world
Make sure to teach them life lessons
Show them exactly how to grow
The second thing you need to do is
Mend fences with friends and family
That have been broken
There is no time to be feuding with anyone
Let the past stay where it's at

Even if it means you being
The bigger person
Make sure to keep your current friends and family close
There is nothing worse than
Falling out with the people that you love the most
Finally
Make sure to tell your wife
You love her a little more often
You married this woman
For a reason
Try whatever it takes
To keep that initial spark burning
Go out on dates
Hold hands while you walk along the lake
Put down that electronic device
For just one second
Show your wife
Just how important
She is in your life
Oh, and before I forget
Try harder to be a better
Son, brother, uncle, nephew, and cousin
You may not see it yet
But there are people who love you
More than you know it
Try to give some of that love back
There you have it
A letter written by you
From the past
Hopefully you took your own advice
And did what this letter said

LETTER TO PAST ME

If you're reading this
You won't believe it
But this letter was written
By you from the future
You wrote this letter
To steer
Yourself away from any misfortunes
That you may encounter
Now you're a big boy
And you're going to do
What you want
But trust yourself on this
There is stuff written in this letter
That will help you out
In the future
First off
There's going to be a girl
Come into your life
But take your friends advice
And don't take the bait
The second thing you need to know

There's going to be a home
That you want to own
Do yourself a favor
And leave it alone
This third thing is important
Read this clear
Don't rack up any student loans
Unless you know
Exactly what degree you're going after
This fourth thing is solid
Read it close
Make sure you save some money
You'll never know
When a surprise might pop up
Finally
This fifth thing is the best
When you meet your wife
Don't rush into it
Date a little while
Get to know each other better
And when it comes time
To pop that big question
Don't forget to ask her father
These five things
Will make your life easier
Take it from yourself kid
Because you're the one
Who wrote this letter

LIES

Do you know
What you want out of life
I'm your friend
You can tell me right
If you tell me your wish
I'll tell you mine
For its not hard to find
This wish of mine
For you're what I want
Out of life
I want to make you laugh
I want to hold you when you cry
I want to be with you
For the rest of my life
I bet you your wish
Is nowhere near mine
In fact, I bet you'll never be mine
We live in two different worlds
We live two different lives
And we call each other friends

Who are we fooling
Why must we live
In our world full of
Lies

LONELY HEART

This lonely heart
Is all alone
Even though
She stands a toe
This lonely heart
Loves her so
In a way
That is unconditional
She stands beside
This lonely heart
Not knowing what he thinks
If only she knew
That this lonely heart
Loves her so
She would see
That this lonely heart
Is none other
Than me

LOST

I can stand
In the rain
To try to erase
All the pain
Or shall I just sit
In the dark
And cry out
Why is it so hard
For me to find my way
I know what direction to go
But instead
I'd rather just stand still
Stuck in my ways
Filled with so much pain
Who would have thought
That I need to be saved
I look fine on the outside
But on the inside
There is nothing but lost
Emptiness

MAKE ME CRY

I never ever told you why
Only your eyes can make me cry
Your personality
Is one of a kind
And that's why girl
Only you can make me cry
I look at you
And I dream I can fly
With you by my side
I always have a good time
You make me feel
All warm inside
That's why girl
Only you
Can make me cry

MEET

Sometimes I wonder
If we were meant to meet
Meeting you
I feel could have been
A curse put onto me
You don't understand how
You make me feel
You don't understand just one of
Two of my biggest fears
My emotions have a tendency
To overwhelm me
But I can control them
Just barely
I like you as a friend
I like you as more
The truth is
I love you a lot more
Then I feel you'll ever know

MIND BLOCK

This writing thing
Usually comes easy to me
But as I sit in this chair
Right here right now
Ideas aren't coming to me so easily
My brain never seems to shut down
But at this second
I think I'm suffering
From mind block
I can't even seem to
Put my pencil to the paper
Without lifting it up
One, two, even three times
Writing poems is my specialty
I think I've finally
Lost my magic touch
Cause I can't even finish
This poem that I started
Without taken a few breaks
This might very well be
The finale poem

You read that
Was written by me
Who am I fooling
I'll never leave
This poem writing alone

INTRO TO MOM

I mentioned in my acknowledgment's that my mom is the strongest women I know. When I sat down to write Mom just as I sat down to write I Can Only See You in My Dreams it took everything in me not to cry. A ton of emotions were hitting me all at once while I was writing this poem. My mom raised my brother and I to be the men we are today. There is no way I can repay her for the things she has done and the things she continues to do for me. I love my mom with every bone in my body. I hope you enjoy reading Mom.

MOM

I love you
In a way I can't explain
You brought me into this world
What else can I say
I might not show it
But it's the truth
You're my mother
And I really do care for you
Whenever you're down
You can turn to me
Your oldest son
For comforting
I'll pick you up
As you've done me
And I'll try to turn
Away all you're gray
There's going to be times
When I'm not there
So, I'll leave you in
Michael's care
I'm sure he'll do

Just as good a job as me
At turning away all you're gray
Mom, I love you in so many ways
I can't begin to tell you
What you mean to me
Keeping me was the best thing
You could have done
Because I'll make sure
You will be proud
Of your oldest son

NEED TO CHANGE

As I was looking
At myself in the mirror today
I realized I didn't like the person
Looking back at me
You see the person
Looking back at me
Has this tendency
To get a little angry
And when that happens
It's not very pretty
Bad word's fly out of my mouth
Sometimes objects get broke
I think it is finally time
To get some help for this problem
Maybe start taking meds
Or talking to somebody
This person in the mirror
Also seems to let loved ones down
Never seems to be around
Always has their own thing going on
Even when they know

About a family event
Well in advance
I think it's time
To mend those fences
Tell those loved ones you miss them
This person in the mirror
Also neglects their health
Is supposed to be going to the gym
Instead they are reaching for the chips
I think it's time
To get serious about this issue
Last thing you want to happen
Is leaving in a hearse
All because you wanted an extra burger
This man in the mirror
Looking back at me
Needs a serious make over
Starting today
But before I change
I must realize
That the man in the mirror
Looking back at me
Is none other than me

NOISE

You take a glance
Over your shoulder
On this cold, dark, rainy night
There is nothing behind you
But you hear this noise
That brings you much fright
You look over your shoulder
Once again
And still nothing is there
But this noise you hear
Is suddenly getting louder
You quickly and loudly
Ask who is there
You get no response
But at that moment
Everything starts to feel so weird
The air is getting heavy
It's so hard to breath
Then that noise
You were hearing
Ends up right in front of you

You see an outline
Of a figure
And it's coming near
You put your fists up
And you holler stay back
The figure is in clear sight now
And it turns out to be
Your best friend
Kicking an aluminum can up the street

NOT EQUAL

I understand your struggle
I feel your pain
We are all supposed to be
Treated equally
But here they beat you
And they call you names
I understand your struggle
I feel your inner pain
Hold on a minute
Here is my rebuttal
You say you understand my struggle
You say you feel my inner pain
Let me ask you a few questions
That's been roaming in my brain
Have you ever lived in poverty
No
Have you ever seen someone
Shot dead that was
Standing right next to you
No
Have you ever been

A victim of a hate crime
No
You answered no
To these three questions
But you clam to understand my struggle
You clam to feel my inner pain
The truth is
We are not the same
But I'm not mad at you
I'm mad at how still
Till this day
People are not treated equally
In this
Land of the Free
Home of the Brave
United States of America
That you and I
Both stay

NOT JUST YOUR BEAUTY

Your beauty is not the only thing I see
To see the real, you
I take a deep look inside of thee
And what I see while I look inside
Is a warm loving person
Someone that truly is kind
A person who'll be there for you
When the time is right
Someone that will love you
And hold you
If you were to cry
Someone who's personality just can't be described
Someone who when you see their
Smile on the outside
It really does shine
All these wonderful qualities I see
When I look
Deep down inside of thee
It's just not your beauty
That I see

You truly are an awesome person
That means a lot to me

NOT THE GIRL FOR ME

I let her get to me
I didn't want to listen
To what anyone had to tell me
I just went out with
Her anyway
Everyone tried to tell me
That she would hurt my heart
And just like they said
She went and tore my heart right out
Everyone tried to tell me
She would just use me
And just like they said
She played me like a game of Yahtzee
Everyone tried to tell me
She wasn't right for me
But I didn't listen to them
I just followed my own lead
I know I messed up big time
By even talking to her
But you better believe
This same thing

Won't happen a second time
I have nothing left to say to her
I'm sure one day
I'll forgive her
Cause I've finally come to see
That she wasn't the girl for me

NOT WHAT IT SEEMS

The American Dream
They tell you
Is to grow up
Get married, buy a house
And have children
So that's exactly what you did
You found the man or woman
Of your dreams
You built a house together
The size of a mansion
You have three kids
They are sweet as can be
But if they told you
Up front that falling into debt
Comes with the American Dream
Would you still take
That deal anyway
You see the American Dream
Is not what it seems
It used to be something
You couldn't wait to get

Something you thought
You couldn't live without
But when you reach your American Dream
And you fall into debt
Living paycheck to paycheck
You scream out
Give me my old life back
I wouldn't trade my kids
Or wife for anything
And maybe I haven't reached
My American Dream yet
But this life right here
With all this debt
Isn't a healthy
Life to live

ONLY BE ME

Light shines off your hair
It even shines off your face
The moon glows bright tonight
As we gaze into
Each other's eyes
This is it
The final and last goodbye
I can't be the man
You're looking for
I can't be the man
To hold you tight
I'm sorry everything happened
The way it did
I completely ripped
Our friendship to shreds
You want me to change
The way that I' am
And to tell you the truth
For you I think I can
But oh well
I'm not what you're looking for

I can only be me
Me who likes you
Me who cares for you
Me who wants to be with you
Me who wants to love you
I'm telling you girl
I can only be me

ONLY SEE YOU

I can see
The bright radiant sparkle in your eyes
I know you would like
To take a trip inside my mind
If you were to take this trip
What do you think you'll find
If you know anything about me
You already know
That I only see you
In my mind
When I close my eyes
You're all I can see
Whenever my eyes are open
If that be day or night
You're the only thing
I can see in my sight
If you would still like
To take that trip inside my mind
Go right ahead
And start visualizing

That I only see you
In my mind

OVER

I see the uncontrollable tears
Roll down your soft cheek
These tears are making your
Big blue eyes puffy
I know the tears you cry
Are because of me
I lied to you once again
And I can see
It's written all over your saddened face
That this is the end
There is nothing I can tell you
Nothing I can buy you
That will make you forgive
Me this time
I'll pack my belongings
And be on my way
I don't deserve an angel from heaven
Like you anyway
I know telling you
I'm sorry
Won't mean a damn thing

I'll just keep
My mouth closed
And walk my pathetic
Feet right out
The front door

PAST TO FUTURE

What would my life be like
If I never got married
What if I would have moved to LA
Like I planned it
If I didn't have kids
Would I be unhappy
What if I didn't finish
My bachelor's degree
And racked up my student loans for nothing
What if I would have
Pulled the trigger that night at the party
What if I never messed around
With that girl in the first place
What if I would have
Moved to Texas
Like my friend asked me to
What if I never got
That speeding ticket
On the way to St. Louis
What if I never left St. Mary's for CSL Behring
What if I had the drive

And determination back then
To write a book
Like I'm doing today
What if I would have
Kept my record label going
What if I never met my sisters
What if I never tried to mend fences with my father
What would have happened
To me if I decided to sell drugs
What if I turned into a
Gangster or a thug
What if I never got into poetry at all
What if I recorded a gospel album
You see I ask all these what if questions
As if my life turned out bad
The fact of the matter is
I wouldn't trade the life that I have
If things would have turned out differently
I may be in jail or dead
I wouldn't have met my wife
And we wouldn't have had our kids
Are there things I would change
If I could go back
I'd be a fool if I'd say no
But I'm not sure
How those changes would have
Altered my future
Changes to my past
Might have made my ego
A little bit bigger
They say everything
Happens for a reason
And I believe that with all my heart
All I can do now
Is let the past be the past
And move on from these what ifs

PERFECT PLACE

I dream of a place
Where the grass is green
The water is blue
And the air is clean
A place where I can
Relax my mind
And let my thoughts run free
A place where I don't have to worry
A place where I don't have to fear
A place where you and I
Can sit and watch the sun go down
Behind the great big hills
A place with no war or violence
A place with just peace and happiness
I wonder if there is a perfect place
Like this
If you happen to be going
To this perfect place
Would you be so kind
To take me with

PICK ME APART

You laugh at the way I dress
You put down my glasses
You say my hair cut
Makes me look stupid
Oh, and the shoes I have on
Make me look like Bozo the clown
All these mean things you say to me
Have you ever stopped to think
About my feelings
Do you ever think
What you're doing to my self-esteem
You're too busy picking me apart
That you don't see
You're tearing me apart
I dress the way I do
Because it expresses who I' am
The glasses I have on
Well the frame belonged
To my deceased grandpa
My deceased grandmother
Used to cut my hair this way

Oh, and as for my shoes
Well they are a tribute
To my father
So, go ahead and continue
To pick me apart
The fact of the matter is
You don't know me at all
You just like making fun of me
I'll pray for you
Because you only pick me apart
For the simple reason
That you're hurting inside
I can see it in your eyes
It's written on your face
But I'll be the bigger person
And I won't make fun of you
Because I don't know what
You're going through

PJR

When your mom
Told me she was pregnant with you
I didn't believe what she was saying
Four years after your sister was born
Surprise baby number two
Which is you
Was going to come into this world
We found out you were a boy
And I jumped for joy
I was going to have a girl and boy
What more could I ask for
Your mom went into labor
While I was at work
I should have rushed to her side
But like a moron I finished my shift
When I arrived at the hospital
Your mom was ready for you to come out
So, I threw some scrubs on
And into delivery I went
You came into this world
Much faster than your older sister

We all were happy to see you
And when you opened your eyes
They were brown just like mine
After your mom and I
Went through a thousand names
We decided to call you Preston James
When we brought you home
Our house was to small
For our family of four
So, we moved to a bigger house
So, you and your sister
Could have your own rooms
We have watched you grow into a young man
Someone who is loving, caring and
Would give you the shirt off their back
I can tell you this son
It's a ruff world out there
Don't let anyone take advantage
Of your kindness
Your mom and I love you very much
And with every day that passes
We are proud that you are our son

PLEASE STAY

I can let you
Walk out that door
But why should I do that
I want you to please stay
You're not happy with me anymore
I'm telling you
We can make it work
If you, please stay
You tell me
That you have found someone else
I'm not mad at you
I just want you
To please stay
You're not in love with me anymore
That's what you yell at me
Well this is my last-ditch effort
With tears running down my eyes
I'll ask you this
One last time
Would you please stay

REWIND TIME

If I could rewind time
I would have met you sooner
We would have fallen in love
When we were younger
We would be living our lives
Happily, every after
If I could rewind time
I'd tell you I love you
Please don't walk out that door
Baby I truly need you
If I could rewind time
We would have grown old together
We would sit on our swing
Holding each other
All while watching our grandchildren
If I could rewind time
I would have tried
To walk up to you
And ask for your number
If only I could
Rewind time

SIMPLE THINGS

It really is the simple things
In life that matter the most
When you're having that bad day at work
And you glance down at your phone
You see a text that has been sent
From your significant other
The text is telling you to hurry home
They have dinner in the oven
And desert will follow
They have arranged
For the kids to be watched
So that the two of you
Can go out and have
A little fun together
They know you like baseball
So, to the game is where you go
You both sing
Take me out to the ball game
At the end of the 7th inning
And you cheer your team to victory
All the way through the bottom of the 9th

And as your walking
To your car after the game
They slowly reach for your hand
And embrace it
You reach your car
Look them deep into
Their eyes
And you thank them
For this evening
Right then and there your
Reminded that it's the
Simple things in life
That matter the most

SOUL

If you looked
Into my soul
What do you think you would see
You could take a quick guess
Maybe build yourself
A desk
But if you investigate this soul
You will find
A big mess
A soul out of place
A soul all alone
A soul that fears no man but God
A soul that needs
To be led home
Does it surprise you
What my soul looks like
What did you think you'd find
A hot air balloon flight
Not in this soul
Not this very night

For all you'll see in this soul
Is a reflection of a man
Whose soul is
Really not in sight

STAND STILL

Your day is always busy
There is always something to do
Whether it be going to work
Picking the kids up from practice
Doing the dishes
Folding the laundry
Or cooking dinner
You are always on the go
Your mind is pulled
In a thousand directions
Most times you don't know
If you're coming or going
And you see
This could drive you crazy
Taking a step back
Giving your mind
Time to relax
Can keep you sane
Almost always
Give it a try one day
Just stand still

And clear your mind
Of all things
Just stand still
And you just might see
That brighter day
You have been looking for

STAY IN LOVE

Can you stay in love
With the one you are with
If this is so
What's the trick
With the temptations
Of others lurking around
How do you keep
Your head above water
If you truly love
The one you're with
You won't need
That genie to grant you
That one wish
To love just one person
Is a tall task
But when you love someone
You should choose to fight
You should choose to never let go
You should choose to stay in love
And try hard
To make that love last

SUPERMAN

The fight is finally over
The dust is finally clearing
Countless towns and a few cities
Have been destroyed
Countless civilians and hero's
Lives have been lost
The two soldiers involved in the battle
Lie motionless on a pile of rubble
One of the soldiers is
A champion for the world
The other soldier was death and destruction
Doomsday was a monster
And it took earths mightiest hero
To take him down
And as Superman lies on the rubble
With Lois Lane holding him in her arms
He looks up at her
And tells her he loves her
With all his heart
As he gets ready to take his last breath
He asks is Doomsday down

Lois with tears flowing
Down her cheek says
Yes, honey you stopped him
And with those final words
Superman passes on

TEARS IN YOUR EYES

I see the tears
Flowing down your cheek
I can tell on this night
Something isn't right
Why are you sad
Is the question I ask
Your heart has been broken
Is what you explain
Broken by someone you love very much
Broken by someone that cheated on you
You don't know if you'll ever stop crying
You're still in shock
That this is all happening
I hand you a tissue
Tell you to wipe your pretty eyes
What happened to you was truly not right
Then I tell you
That you deserve better
You look up at me
Tears still in your eyes
And gently say really

I say yes
Anyone that would cheat on you
Don't deserve your beauty
A smile comes across your warm face
As you softly say thanks
I tell you no problem
If you don't mind
I'll just sit right here beside you
The tears that were in your eyes
Are there no longer
We sit and talk through the night
The moon shines bright
And I think to myself
This could be the start of
Something great

THAT NIGHT

I saw you from across the room
Dancing with your girlfriends
Oh man you dance smooth
Then one of your girlfriends
Came up to me
And tapped me on the shoulder
She told me you wanted to dance with me
I couldn't believe it
Cause to me you were the finest
Thing I had ever seen
I walked over to you
And asked for your hand
You put your hand in my
And I led you to the dance floor
We danced and laughed all through the night
And when the club was ready to close
We just held each other tight
You softly kissed me on the check
And said you had to go
You left without us exchanging numbers
So now I have no idea

How to get a hold of you
A few weeks later
I'm out at the same club
And across the room on the dance floor I spot you
We suddenly lock eyes and I stroll over to see you
We embrace and begin dancing
Picking up where we left off
It's the end of the night once again
This time I ask for your number
And you write it on my hand
I call the next day
To set up our official first date
This could be the start of something big
I can't wait to see where this all ends up

THE ONE

You start out
On your own
With nothing to do
And nowhere to go
You buy a house
On your own
With nothing to move in
Nothing to show
You go to work
Five days a week
You make some money
But you have no one to treat
Until that day
You meet the one
The women of your dreams
Comes into your life
Just like a ray of sun
You settle down
You have some kids
You spend the rest of your life
With this woman

The women that makes you happy
The women that makes you smile
The women that makes you angry
The women you
Just can't live without

THINGS AREN'T THE SAME

Things just aren't the same
Well you're right
The reason things aren't the same
Is because we had
Another big fight
Just last night
A lot of harsh words
Came flying out of our mouths
The screaming and yelling
All came to a sudden halt
When I punched a hole
In our living room wall
With tears flowing
Down your smooth cheek
You softly whispered
Goodbye to me
Then it felt like everything
Was moving in slow motion
As you turned
And walked away from me

Things just aren't the same
And now I finally see
That I may have lost
You forever all because
Of my own stupidity

TORN

It doesn't matter
How hard I try
I just can't seem
To get you out of my mind
I'm torn between two people
William and Billy
But come to find out
Both people are me
William wants you to let him be
Billy wants you to stay
My mind divides me
My heart wants nothing but peace
I just can't make you see
You're the only one for me
And there's no place
I'd rather be
Than with you
Holding you tight
As you sleep
At night

TRAVEL THE WORLD

Let's take a trip around the world
How does Paris sound to you
We can check out the Eiffel Tower
Have a romantic dinner for two
Then we can hop on down to Italy
Take a ride on a gondola
Visit the Vatican
Look up at the Sistine Chapel
We can swing on up to Great Britain
Say hi to the Queen
Take a trip down under
And visit Sydney
We can go on an African Safari
We can even go to Jamaica
To learn a little more about Bob Marley
We can walk a top the Great Wall of China
See the Sphinx in Egypt
The Taj Mahal in India
There's the Mayan Ruins in Mexico
Saint Basil's Cathedral in Moscow

All these wonderful things
Are spread across the world
I'd like to visit these places
With only you
My one true love

TURN YOUR BACK

You've been working so hard
You made it this far
The finish line is right there
Why did you stop
You started listening to others
That said you couldn't do it
So, you turned your back
On all your goals
All because someone
Told you that you're crazy
All your blood sweat and tears
That you put into this
You're just going to up and quit
Because of some nonsense
I don't understand
You got so much talent
You have such a great plan
Don't turn your back
Because of a negative person
Keep grinding for what you believe in

I can see that you want this
I can see the eye of the tiger
Burning in your eyes
Just don't turn your back
On any of your dreams

TYPES OF FRIENDS

You calm to have many friends
When you're down and out
How many of your friends
Will help you out
Many friends clam to have your back
When your backs against the wall
How many of your friends
Will join in your fight
There are two types of friends
The normal friend
And the true friend
The normal friend
Will talk you up
But when you're down and out
And you look up
The normal friend
Won't be around
The true friend
Will wipe the tears
From your eyes
When you cry

They will tell you what
You need to hear
And not make up some lie
You see the difference
Between a normal friend and true friend
Is clear
The question is
Which type of friends
Will you draw nearer

UNCONDITIONAL THOUGHTS

It's whatever you want
It's whatever sets you free
Its unconditional thoughts
It's you and me
You can be down
You can be out
But unconditional thoughts
Can wipe away your frown
When darkness falls
And it starts to rain
Your unconditional thoughts
Can bring you sun rays
Unconditional thoughts
It can be whatever you want
All you must do
Is clear your mind
And think positive
Unconditional thoughts

WHAT WOULD LIFE BE LIKE

Do you sometimes
Just close your eyes
Let your mind wander
Wander off to a place
Where the grass is greener
Just close your eyes and imagine
What life would be like
If you lived somewhere further
Just close your eyes
And imagine being smarter
If your life were different
Would you be happy
Would you be on cloud nine
Always tap dancing
Or would you be sad and lonely
Would all your friends
Just use you for your money
You see we all might want different lives
But should we wish for things
That could make drive us crazy
I'm not saying if you're unhappy to stay content with your life

Make a change in your life
That will hopefully be for the better
What would life be like
If you were to make a change
There is only one way to find out
You'll have to find that way
All by yourself

WHAT WENT WRONG

We don't laugh anymore
To say I love you
Seems like a chore
If you were to ask me
To hold your hand
I'd just ignore the fact
That you had asked
Somewhere along the line
Our relationship derailed
We fell out of love
Neither of us even care
We've just fallen into a routine
We do the same thing everyday
You play on your phone
While I just watch the game
Every now and then
We ask each other
How was your day
But those days are few and far between
How did this happen
What went wrong with our relationship

We used to hug each other everyday
Now we just yell at each other
And call each other names
Why do we hang on
If our love for each other is gone
How come neither one of us
Can walk out that door
And call it quits forever
Is there still a glimmer of hope for us
Can we turn this bus around
I can only speak for myself
And I want to try and work this out
I married you because I love you
That has never changed for me
I feel we got comfortable
Just going through the motions
We must take it back to day one
When we first met
We both saw that spark
In each other's eyes
We both never wanted to leave the others side
We told each other I love you
Each and everyday
I held your hand
I would rub your feet
There was no doubt in either of our minds
That we weren't meant to be
So, let's spice things up
I'm willing to try if you are
I want my wife back
I want to love you with all my heart
If we try and it don't work
Well then, we can go our separate ways
But I'm at least willing to fight
To save our marriage

WHAT YOU'VE MADE ME

I can be your best friend
Or I can be your enemy
I can make you love me
Or I'll make you hate me
You see I'm
Whatever you make me
This for you could be a good thing
Or a bad thing
I consider myself a nice person
Right up until you cross me
You see I've already told you
I'm what you make me
I really don't get too upset
I keep myself humbled
And for the most part
I'm blessed
The one thing that's for sure about me is
I'm what you've made me

WISHFUL THINKING

I close my eyes and I dream of
You and I hand in hand
The ocean waves grazing our feet
The sea shells as fruitful as our conversation
The breeze accompanied
The smell of the sea
Why does it have to be a crisp and exhilarating dream
Just a thought in my head
A dream I dreamt often
The beginning of our love story
As I open my eyes and reality
Floods back in washing away the
Wishful thinking of us
And the rare and incredible love
We could have

WORDS

Words can cut like a knife
Words can tear a person
Right down to smurf size
Words can be harsh
Words can be dangerous
But words can also be kind
Words can be gentle
Words can be loving
Words can stick with you
Words can't be taken back
And that's an honest fact
The ongoing life mystery
About words will live on
Beyond the end of time
So, choose your words wisely
And try to stay humble and kind

WOULD YOU MIND

Would you mind
If I attempted to captivate your heart
Discover what makes it tick
Would you mind
If I were to unearth your soul
To learn all your aspirations
And unparalleled charisma
Would you mind if I were your admirer
Would you mind
If I'm cautious and unpretentious
Expressing my affection for you
Would you mind if I wanted
To promise to keep you company for a lifetime
Never take for granted our daily benign moments
Would you mind if I told you
I cherish everything about you
From your charming beauty
To your clever come backs
There is nothing in this whole wide world
That I want from you

And there is nothing I expect you to give
But there is one thing I'd like to know
Would you mind
If someday maybe
I could hold your hand

WOULD YOU MIND PART 2

Would you mind
If I would take you out and show you around
Show you my home town and what I'm all about
Would you mind
If I let my heart spill out onto your lips
Would you mind
If while walking hand in hand
I was to expose my love to you
My love for you runs deep
You have taking my heart to uncharted waters
My mind is still trying to catch up
Would you mind
Staying awhile
I want to know all your dreams and ambitions
I could immerse myself in your existence
Would you mind
If I took you places
Both of us experiencing the journey together
Would you mind
Letting me support you during your
Suffering and celebrate in your triumphs

Would you mind
Being my life long ally
My Juliet
In this ever-changing world
Would you mind

YOU'RE IN CHARGE

You're in charge of your life
Not your mom's expectations
Not your dad's aspirations
Not your brother's interest
Not your sister's legacy
Not your aunt's traditions
Not even your uncle's ambitions
You're in charge of how your story is written
Your fate is to be decided by you
Stop letting others determine your future
Be courageous
Stay fierce in your beliefs
When friends become foes
Life's obstacles will expose your allies
That is when you are truly
Capable to channel your worth
And take charge
In declaring your destiny

YOU'RE THE GIRL

You're the girl
I dreamt about every night
The perfect girl
I'd cherish and hold tight
The girl
If my spirit was destroyed
Your presence could rejuvenate me
And remedy my mind
You're the girl
With the savory disposition
Your unspoken love
Can turn away my anguish
But you're also the girl
That can be so numb to my affliction
The girl
That evokes others despair
The girl
That everyone respects
Even if it's undeserving
You shut everyone out
Because you crave the attention

From the backlash of your malicious ways
You're the girl
I became infatuated with
The one I lusted over
Although I see now
You're the girl that don't deserve my love
So why are you still the girl
I fantasize about

ABOUT THE AUTHOR

Will Rasmussen has been writing poetry since he was fourteen years old. He writes poems about everyday life issues he has dealt with. He has written poems that will make you laugh, cry and think. He has written poems about such issues as love, friendship, marriage, loneliness, happiness, and death. His mission is that the reader will somehow someway relate to what he has written and take something from the poems that may help them if they may be going through something. Everything he writes is all original and comes straight from his heart. He is married with three kids. He graduated Summa Cum Laude from Rasmussen College with his bachelor's degree in Business Management. He is co-owner of a business called Memorable Apparel with his good friend Richie Winston. This is his first book that he has released.